Foreword

Tired of the bride trying to convince you that "Love Can Build a Bridge" by The Judds is an appropriate and effective bridal processional (and sounds lovely as a trumpet solo)? Looking for appropriate "stretch" music when the minister is running late?

Then this book is for you.

In the collective freelance careers of the members of this group, we've likely played millions of weddings. And each one was a musical masterpiece. The pages that follow will teach you how to make your performance equally as spectacular… or at least make the experience of planning and playing music for a wedding less stressful for you and for the bride.

All kidding aside, weddings are important day for the people involved and should be handled as such. We have compiled the most frequently requested and frequently played music for each portion of the ceremony. Musical options are organized in the order most likely performed, with several options for prelude, processional and recessional. The arrangements are from our own personal library and are made easy to read, allowing you, the performer, freedom to pay attention to the needs of the ceremony.

Once you've used this book a couple of times, I'm sure "Insert Title Here" will become a standard in your repertoire.

-Chuck Daellenbach

Prelude
The prelude sets the tone for the ceremony to follow, so the music chosen should be beautiful and tranquil. We suggest either Canon (Pachelbel), Prayer from *Hansel and Gretel* (Humperdinck), Largo from *Xerxes* (Handel), Air from *Water Music* (Handel) or Air on the G String from *Suite No. 3* (Bach).

Processionals
For most weddings you will need music for three processionals: the mothers' entrance, the bridal party, and the bride.

For the mothers' entrance, something light, similar to the prelude music, is appropriate. Pachelbel's "Canon" or Bach's "Air on the G Sting" are our recommendations and are the selections which are most often requested.

For the bridal party, the musical tone begins to shift, setting a grander mood. Purcell's "Trumpet Tune," Clarke's "Trumpet Voluntary," and Stanley's "Trumpet Voluntary" are our favorites.

The big moment has arrived. To announce the bride's entrance, we have included the famous "Albason Fanfare." For her processional, the most common requests are the Clarke "Trumpet Voluntary" and Wagner's "Bridal Chorus." However, the pieces by Purcell and Stanley are also options. Though less commonly used, Monteverdi's "Orfeo Fanfare" is completely appropriate.

Recessional
The recessional should mark the joyous beginning of the new couple's life together. Mendelssohn's "Wedding March," Mouret's "Rondeau" and the "Orfeo Fanfare" are preferred for this occasion. Stanley's "Trumpet Voluntary" may be used as well for the recessional.

"AIR"
from *Water Music*

Handel
(1685-1759)
Arranged by Walter Barnes

LARGO

from *Xerxes*

George Frideric Handel
(1685-1759)
arranged by Walter Barnes

UBA

PRAYER
from *Hansel and Gretel*

TUBA

Engelbert Humperdinck
(1854-1921)
arranged by Henry Charles Smith

Andante con moto ♩ = 69

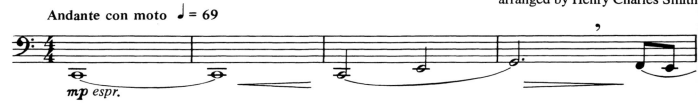

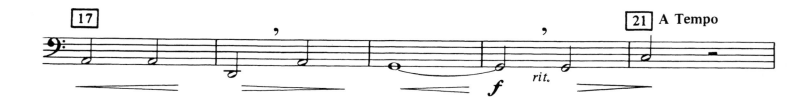

AIR ON THE G STRING
from Suite No. 3

J. S. Bach
(1685–1750)
Trans. by A. Frackenpohl

Tuba

CANON

Johann Pachelbe
(1653-1706
arranged by Walter Barne

6

TUBA

FANFARE
from ORFEO

Tuba

Claudio Monteverdi
(1567-1643)
adapted and arranged by Stephen McNeff

TRUMPET TUNE AND AYRE

Henry Purce
(1659-169
arranged by Walter Barne

TUBA

9

TRUMPET VOLUNTARY

Stanley
(1713-1786)
arranged by Walter Barnes

2003, 1986, Canadian Brass Publications LTD
International Copyright Secured

Trumpet Voluntary *continued*

TRUMPET VOLUNTARY

Jeremiah Clarke
(1673-1707)
arranged by Walter Barnes

TUBA

2003, 1988, Canadian Brass Publications LTD
International Copyright Secured

BRIDAL CHORUS
from LOHENGRIN

Richard Wagner
(1813-1883)
edited by Canadian Brass

Tuba

WEDDING MARCH

Tuba

Felix Mendelssohn
(1809–1847)
Adapted by Ryan Anthony

RONDEAU
(Theme from *Masterpiece Theatre*)

Jean-Joseph Mouret
(1682-1738)
arranged by Walter Barnes

TUBA

OTHER APPROPRIATE WEDDING PIECES

Prelude
Fantasie (Bach)
Sheep May Safely Graze (Bach)*
Where e'er you walk (Handel)*

Prelude or Solo
Bist du bei mir (Bach, attr.)

Prelude or Processional
Jesu, Joy of Man's Desiring from *Cantata 147* (Bach)
Wachet auf (Sleepers Awake) from *Cantata 140* (Bach)*

Processional or Recessional
Trumpet Voluntary (Boyce)
Prelude from *Te Deum* (Charpentier)
March (Allegro spiritoso) from *Heroic Suite* (Telemann)

Solo
Ave Maria (Bach/Gounod)
Ave Maria (Schubert)

Recessional
Ode to Joy (Beethoven)
Allegro from *Water Music* (Handel)*
Arrival of the Queen of Sheba from *Solomon* (Handel)*
La Rejouissance (The Rejoicing) from *Music for the Royal Fireworks* (Handel)

More Recommended Music for Weddings
My heart ever faithful from *Cantata 68* (Bach)
Pavane (Fauré)
Pie Jesu from *Requiem, Op. 48* (Fauré)
Panis Angelicus (Franck)
Let the Bright Seraphim from *Samson* (Handel)*
Psalm XIX: The Heavens Declare (Marcello)
Toccata (Martini)
Alleluia from *Exsultate, jubilate* (Mozart)*
Ave verum corpus (Mozart)*
Agnus Dei (Palestrina)
Sonata for Two Trumpets and Brass (Purcell)*
Concerto in C (Vivaldi)*

*Canadian Brass publications